A History of Haxby

Tom Smith

William Sessions Limited
The Ebor Press
York, England

First published 1988
© Tom Smith 1988
ISBN 1 85072 037 1

Printed by
William Sessions Limited
The Ebor Press
York, England

For Brenda

Contents

List of Maps

List of Plates

Acknowledgements

My thanks are due to the following for their help in compiling this history.

Miss Susan Bellerby, Mrs. Norah Rushton and the Haxby Branch Library for unrestricted access to information in their possession. Mr. Holmes of the Ryedale District Council, for information covering the housing development in the parish. Ms. Edna Coleman for producing the maps and some of the photographs.

Publication has been assisted by a grant from the Sheldon Memorial Trust.

Preface

In his excellent book, *Writing Local History*, David Dymond urges anyone attempting the task to ask themselves why they are doing so. My reason is very simple. In 1970, I arrived as a "foreigner" to the parish shortly before the large housing estates were built to handle the influx of new residents. As a result, I was able to experience and enjoy the character of Haxby before the watershed years of the early '70s, and to observe the pressures that development has placed on the village, its architecture, farmland and wildlife since then. My purpose is to record what went before to make the Haxby of today, and what exists today before it, too, is displaced.

Being a comparative newcomer, I have no claim to be motivated by nostalgia, although many of the losses the village has sustained even in my time as a resident seem regrettable. My standpoint is probably best expressed by the spirit in which the conservation order for the centre of Haxby was made in 1976. Whilst accepting the inevitable changes that the growth in population must bring, the document asserts that there is little or no potential for building in the designated area and that any development which does take place should conserve the existing buildings. It also directs that any infilling should be of brick structures with red clay pantile roofs and no more than two storeys high. It is difficult to equate what has happened since then in the village centre, and what is still happening, with the terms of the conservation order.

Haxby has a thousand years of history, much of which is to be found in historical archives but an important part of which is still to be read in its existing fabric. It would surely be a disservice to future villagers if we failed to preserve what, of value, still exists.

CHAPTER I

Introduction

The township of Haxby was founded in the ancient Forest of Galtres by Danish settlers about 1,000 years ago. At that time, the forest covered a fan-shaped area spreading northwards from the city of Jorvik (York). Its eastern boundary was defined by the river Derwent, its western boundary by the upper Ouse and Swale and to the north it petered out on the higher and drier slopes of what are now known as the Hambleton and Howardian hills.

The land on which it grew was generally marshy, comprising a light sandy soil overlaying heavy deposits of clay laid down after the ice age, and was inefficiently drained by the river Foss and its tributaries which flow approximately north to south. The terrain rarely rose higher than fifty feet above sea level and supported a mixture of deciduous trees including birch, brushwood and many fine oaks. The density of the forest varied from dark areas of tall trees, through marshy brushwood to grassy clearings, and was ideal to support a varied wildlife. As well as a wealth of small game, the fauna included bears, wolves, wild boar and deer and the presence of the more ferocious animals meant that early inhabitants of the area generally gave the forest a wide birth. A reasonable impression of how the forest must have looked can still be gained from certain parts of Strensall Common, in particular in the nature reserve on the north side of the railway line. The pathway winds through a mixture of bogland, birch and brushwood with occasional oaks and patches of grazing.

The first inhabitants of the area about which there are any significant historical records were the ancient British tribes of the Parisi and Brigantes. Their settlements skirted the forest, and the Brigantes' capital, Isurion, is thought to have stood on the site of present day Aldborough. To the south of Isurion was a small, unimportant township on the Ouse called Caer Abrauc which was destined to become the city of York. The name was formerly thought to mean the

1

city of King Ebraucus, but is now believed to mean the place of yew trees. Very few Ancient British place names have survived in the area, Crayke (Krakjo = a rock) and Alne being two rare examples. On the other hand, the names of a number of rivers can be traced back to the times of the Brigantes, for instance Kyle meaning narrow, Derwent meaning either oak-lined or white or clear water, and Ouse meaning water.

The Ancient Britons used the higher, firmer ground surrounding the forest to support a road system linking their settlements. By 70 AD, the Romans had invaded the area and driven out the British. They incorporated the old road system into their national network by the addition of characteristically long, straight links and chose Caer Ebrauc as their headquarters, renaming it Eboracum. Over the years they established it as capital of the province of Britannia Inferior and a key military, administrative and commercial centre.

Under the Romans, the forest continued to be avoided except as a natural source for timber and game and no road was driven directly north through it from Eboracum. Two routes, however, were cut through the less dense sections. One ran northwest from York to Shipton and then north to Easingwold and on to Thirsk. The other, ran from Brough on the Humber to cross the Derwent at Stamford Bridge, then passed through Sheriff Hutton before joining the Thirsk road at Easingwold. Map A combines information from several sources to illustrate the road system surrounding the forest at the end of the Roman occupation.

Early in the 5th century, the Romans withdrew their legions and invaders from Saxony, Jutland and Friesland moved in to fill the power vacuum. By 627, the remaining Romano-British inhabitants had been slaughtered or enslaved and Edwin had become Anglo Saxon king of all England except Kent. Eboracum had been renamed Eoforwic and, as well as being Edwin's capital, it was capital of the English province of Deira and its ecclesiastical centre. Before the end of the century under the influence of Alcuin, the city was second only to Rome as a centre of learning.

For the first time townships began to be established within the Forest of Galtres and the area where Haxby parish was later to develop lay between the Anglo Saxon townships of Sutton on Forest, Strensall, Earswick, Huntington and Haxby's future close neighbour, Wigginton. More specifically, part of its eastern boundary was to be determined by the river Foss whose name was derived from the Roman word fossa, meaning a ditch.

2

Map A

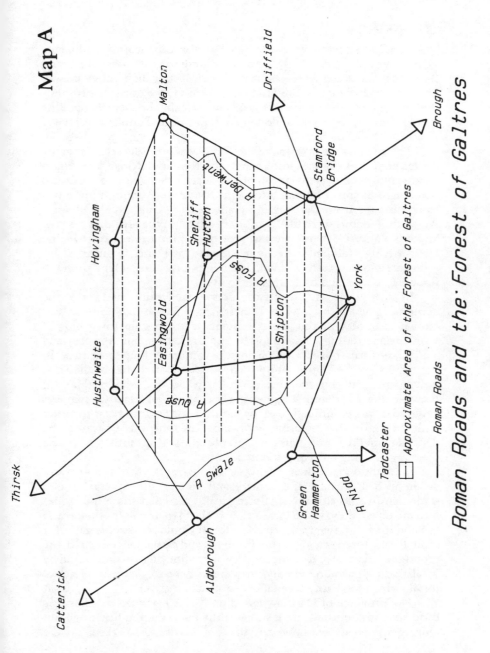

Malton

Driffield

Hovingham

Sheriff Hutton

Stamford Bridge

R Derwent

Brough

Thirsk

Husthwaite

Easingwold

R Foss

Shipton

York

R Ouse

R Swale

Catterick

Aldborough

Green Hammerton

R Nidd

Tadcaster

☐ Approximate Area of the Forest of Galtres

—— Roman Roads

Roman Roads and the Forest of Galtres

3

THE VIKINGS

In AD 865 a further wave of invaders, this time from Scandinavia, swept over the country. After years of raiding the east coast of Britain, the Danes occupied East Anglia and then began their move inland. Using the waterways of the Humber and the Ouse to make progress, they overran Eoforwic in AD 866. Once again the city changed its name, this time to Jorvik, but retained its position of importance; it was now capital of Danelaw.

The effect of the invasion of the Danes was quite different from the earlier arrival of the Anglo Saxons. The Romano-British and Anglo Saxon cultures had been entirely alien to each other whereas the Danes and Anglo Saxons had much more in common. Although there was stiff resistance from the Anglo Saxons in some parts of the country which the Vikings were finally to succumb to, in the area that we now know as Yorkshire their arrival was relatively bloodless. In AD 876, the Danish King Halfdan shared out the land of Danelaw amongst his followers and they settled down, often on poorer soils or land prone to flooding, to farm and trade in order to live.

In many places the newcomers were assimilated into the community cheek by jowl with their Anglo Saxon neighbours. Well known examples of this close existence are the twin townships of Uppleby and Easingwold, Helperby and Brafferton, and Sowerby and Thirsk; the former in each pair being the younger Viking settlement. In the same way, the Danes set up townships on both banks of the Foss, Towthorpe between the river and Earswick, and Haxby (Haxebi) between the river and Wigginton. The origin of Haxby's name is believed to be a combination of the family name Hakr or Haac together with the suffix -by denoting township. Towthorpe is belived to be derived from the family name of Tofi plus the still apt suffix of -thorpe meaning outlying farm or settlement.

In addition to their prowess as mariners, the Danes were accomplished farmers and traders and so the site of Haxby as a settlement would suit their culture ideally. Situated some four miles into the forest, they would have ample fuel and materials for shelter and to build road and river transport. The forest would also supply game for food, forage for pigs and pasture for sheep and cattle. Once cleared, the ground was fertile for farming, and the neighbouring villages would be ideal trading partners. Finally, they were close to the Viking city of Jorvik, which was easily accessible overland or by river.

The province of Danelaw lasted until AD 954 when its ruler Eric Bloodaxe was defeated and it was absorbed into the English kingdom. During its existence, however, the boundaries of Yorkshire were established to last for over a thousand years and the old Anglo Saxon areas known as hundreds were replaced by the Danish wapentakes. One of these was the Wapentake of Bulmer, which contained the Forest of Galtres, and within the forest lay the newly-founded village of Haxby.

The English kingdom came to an end in 1066 with the battle of Hastings. However, the seeds of Harold's defeat were sown earlier that year, just a few miles from Haxby, at Stamford Bridge. It was there that Harold met and defeated his rebel brother Tostig but immediately had to return to the south to face William's invasion at Hastings. The English army arrived weary and unprepared for combat, while William's forces were rested and organised. By mid October, Harold had been killed in battle and the Normans occupied England.

THE NORMANS

William the Conqueror viewed his new acquisition as a vast source of revenue, each unit of which had to be assessed and managed. He set about the task of management by allocating areas to his noblemen and to those important Anglo Saxons who gave him their allegiance, but in such a way as to ensure that none of them had a sufficient number of contiguous areas to enable them to create their own rival kingdom. In Yorkshire, the land was divided between some thirty principal tenants including the king himself, Robert, Count of Mortain, who was the king's half-brother, and Count Alan, the king's son-in-law. One other notable tenant was the Anglo Saxon Archbishop of York who had either total or shared interest in numerous townships amongst which were Skelton, Earswick, Towthorpe, Strensall, Flaxton, Wigginton and Haxby itself.

The assessment for taxation was done by the compilation of Domesday Book in 1086. The entry for Haxby affords the first opportunity to focus on the village in its own right and from its sparse details plus knowledge of the history of the time, a sketch of the early days of Haxby can be created. Domesday records that Haxby was owned, before and after the Conquest, by the Archbishop of York. At the time of the Conquest Ealdred was Archbishop, and he it was who crowned William in Westminster Abbey on Christmas Day 1066. Ealdred died in 1069 and was succeeded by the Norman Thomas of Bayeux who held the position at the time Domesday was compiled and until his death in 1100.

For tax purposes Haxby was assessed as six carucates and one bovate, or six and one eighth carucates. Since a carucate could be anything from 120 to 240 acres, it is not possible to deduce exatly how big the parish of Haxby was at that time. However, it is generally accepted for this area that a figure of 120 should be assumed, in which case, the size of the parish would have been 735 acres. Domesday further records that there were seven villagers with three ploughs; a villager in this case meaning someone of the peasant class who owned a significant amount of land. The value of the parish was 20s. in 1086, while its value before 1066 was estimated as 40s. This drop in value was the result of William's punitive campaigns against the rebellious northerners in the intervening years.

In 1068 and 1069, the king had to lead armies into Northumbria to quell uprisings against his tenants, and this he did with great savagery. The military operation is known as the harrying or devastation of the north. Few townships escaped being burned to the ground along with their crops, while the populace and livestock were put to the sword. By comparison with many places, Haxby either avoided William's worst excesses or recovered remarkably quickly. Stillington for example was worth 40s. before devastation but only 10s. in 1086, Strensall was described as "waste" while Wigginton was termed "was and is waste".

HAXBY WITHIN THE FOREST OF GALTRES

From the 13th century onwards Haxby begins to be mentioned specifically in various records and it is possible to see it emerging as a village with its own individuality. In 1227, the court rolls of St. Peter of York record the resolution of a long-standing dispute between the men of Haxby on the one hand and Robert, son of Maldred and his predecessor Henry de Neville on the other. For the sum of forty marks from Walter de Wisebec and John Romayn, canons of Driffield and Strensall, Robert relinquished his rights over an unspecified acreage bounded by Ellerpittes, Redker, Houkeshill, Under Houkeshill and Grenthwait. Unfortunately, this area cannot be identified today.

Because it was a royal possession from Norman times, the monarch of the day made generous gifts of venison and timber to those who had earned reward or required favour. By the end of 12th century, the size of the forest had been significantly reduced. The western boundary had withdrawn to the River Kyle and its eastern limit to the River Foss, while to the north it went little further than Easingwold. At this point, the forest was divided into three bailiwicks known as Kyle, Easingwald and Myrescough. In 1295, Haxby was probably in the Bailiwick of Myrescough along with Strensall, Huntington and Earswick. The depredations continued unabated so that by 1400, the

6

three bailiwicks had been reduced to two, North and South, with Haxby in the South Bailiwick.

The relative size of Haxby to its neighbours can be assessed to some degree by inspecting the taxation records of the time. In 1301, the Lay Subsidy for Edward I lists twenty-four heads of families in Haxby as being taxed for a total amount of £5; by comparison, Wigginton's total was 30s. 4d., while Towthorpe, Huntington, Easingwold, Skelton and Heworth were all taxed as one. The Lay Subsidy of 1334 valued Haxby at £1 13s. 4d., compared with Wigginton at 10s., Strensall at £1 16s., Sutton on the Forest at £1 10s. and Huntington at 18s. In 1377 a Poll Tax on the whole population of England aged fourteen and over was levied at 4p. per head. The returns for Haxby cum Welynton (Haxby and Wigginton combined) show that the number of people taxed was 167, while for Huntington and Towthorpe the number was 93 and for Strensall 47.

Among the taxpayers listed in 1301 returns was a certain Thomas Westiby who will appear again in the story of Haxby as the unwitting instrument by which the village finally got its own burial ground in 1328.

The participation of Haxby in the judicial process in the forest is illustrated by several entries in the Calender of Patent Rolls. The haywarden of the forest in 1279 was John de Wiresdale and in that year he held an inquisition on the death of William Gryvel, a mounted forester. By oath of representatives "of the townships of Galtres Forest, that is to say, Esingwalde, Hoby [Huby], Sutton, Stivelington [Stillington], Ferlington [Farlington], Strensall, Haxeby, Wyginton and Neuton", Gryvel's occupation and status were confirmed. In 1357 another inquisition heard the complaint of John de Wynewyk that the steward of the forest was threatening to change the course of a stream which, since time immemorial, had flowed through de Wynewyk's land and driven his mill at Alne. The Haxby represenative was William Abell who, along with other "good men resident in the same forest", found in favour of de Wynewyk.

The general impression of justice in the middle ages is that it was rough and summary; two examples from the Calenders of Patent Rolls for 1345 and 1393 paint a more benign picture. In 1345, an intriguing incident occurred which eventually drew the royal family of the day into the conflict. William le Clere of Haxby and his wife, Cicely, were convicted of various thefts in the village and in Huntington, including breaking into Huntington church. They were convicted and sentenced to death. However, Cicely was both pregnant and a friend of Queen Phillipa and these two factors combined to get a pardon from Edward

III. The second example is an entry for 1393 in which Thomas Raper of Haxby was pardoned for the theft of two oxen from his fellow villager Robert Godebarn.

Not all wrong-doers recorded in the Patent Rolls escaped so lightly however. In 1433 Haxby men were involved in two gangs who appeared to terrorise the area. Each gang numbered a dozen or more men drawn from several townships and apparently under the leadership of a William Shupton of Shupton (Shipton), described as "gentilman". The first, which included Robert Brok of Haxby, attacked the property in Spaunton and Hornse of William, Abbot of St. Mary's, York, stole cattle, game and fish and threatened his servants and monks in Tollerton and Shupton. The second gang, containing Henry Abell and Robert Raper of Haxby, made similar attacks on the same abbot's "close at Bothum". Both groups were heavily fined.

In his *History of Easingwold and the Forest of Galtres*, G. C. Cowling lists specific references to Haxby and neighbouring villages from the records of forest management. In 1538 Haxby was required to pay the Justice of the Forest an annual fee of 3s., while Wigginton and Sutton on Forest each had to pay the Master of Game 13s. 4d. for various rights such as browsing and pannage. The Master of Game also collected a payment of 38s. 8d. on the last day of the "fence month", of which Haxby's part was 4s., Wigginton's 3s. 4d. and Strensall's a mere 1s.

In 1620, Thomas Lumsden became Master of Game and left detailed records of the state of the forest in the reign of James I. In 1625, the stock of deer was estimated as 803 and the size of the woodland by 1630 was down to 7,600 acres. Enclosures by licence from the king were steadily reducing the forest and trespass and poaching by the inhabitants were rife. In 1629, Charles I decided to boost his ailing exchequer by capitalising on his ownership of the forest. In 1630 he set in hand the process of disafforestation which was completed by the end of the year. The arrangements meant that Haxby received 1277 acres to add to its parish, an allotment third only in size to Easingwold's (1776) and Sutton on Forest's (1500).

The final happening of note during this period was the siege of York during the Civil War which is described in detail in L. P. Wenham's *The great and close Siege of York*. From mid-April 1644, for five weeks, the Parliamentary forces had beseiged Royalist York and mopped up their strongholds at Crayke, Buttercrambe, Stamford Bridge and elsewhere. In his attempt to raise the seige, Prince Rupert brought his troops from Lancashire down the east bank of the Swale and, according to his own journal, spent the night of 1st July "in Galres

8

woode", in the vicinity of Skelton. But that was as close as the war came to Haxby because from there Rupert crossed the Ouse to surprise the enemy with an attack from the west.

CHAPTER II

Development of the Parish

The modern day boundaries of the parish were basically established as late as 1630 by the act of disafforestation. Today, the parish is bounded on the east by the Foss and its northern tributary, Golland Dike, which form the border with Strensall and Huntington parishes. To the north it shares a boundary with Sutton on Forest and on the south and west, respectively with the parishes of Earswick and Wigginton.

Typically, a parish is expected to have a church and a manor house; atypically, Haxby originally had neither and, even more unusually, it was divided between two manors. In addition, the chapel was a "peculiar" which means it was not part of any diocese and therefore did not pay dues to a diocesan bishop. Instead, it seems to have been responsible from both an ecclesiastic and administrative point of view to the Archbishop of York.

THE MANOR

As recorded in Domesday, Haxby was owned by the Archbishop of York both before and after the Norman Conquest. In 1223, Haxby men in custody for trespass in the forest were described as being "of the Dean and Chapter", and in 1328, the villagers were referred to as belonging "from of old" to the prebendaries of Strensall and Driffield. A prebend is a payment from the revenues of a cathedral to a canon and a prebendary is the recipient of the payment.

There is no definite record of when the parish became the property of these two prebendaries. The *Victoria County History* (VCH) states that the first recorded appointments to the prebends were in 1235 for Driffield and 1279 for Strensall. However, the record in *Early Yorkshire Charters* of the settlement of the dispute with Robert, son of Maldred, ends with the comment that Walter de Wisebeck and John Romayn, canons of York, paid 40 marks in settlement of Robert's claim; this being in 1227. Furthermore, within the same entry, the territory is defined as "from the place where the cross stood in the days of . . . Nicholas de Trailli and Hugh Murdac, canons of York . . . " It seems likely that these two were being referred to as prebendaries for Strensall and Driffield, and if so, de Trailli was the incumbent in 1167.

The parish was split into East End Manor (Driffield prebend), and West End Manor (Strensall prebend). At the time of the Enclosure Act in 1769, the prebendary for the Driffield parcel of the village was Rev. William Mason and his lessee and Lord of the East End Manor was Samuel Waud. The prebendary for the Strensall parcel was Rev. Thomas Hurdis (DD) whose lessee and Lord of the West End Manor was Sir William Robinson, Bart.

In 1835, in an attempt to reorganise and strengthen the finances of the Church of England, the Ecclesiastical Commissioners were set up. The ownership of the two manors passed into the hands of the Commissioners, and they later sold the church's rights to the lessees of the time. East End Manor was bought by Edward Wande and the West End Manor was bought by Leonard Thompson. By 1865, however, the East End Manor had again changed hands, this time being bought for £775 by a York solicitor called Hodgson. This was a surname which was to become very prominent in village affairs in the latter part of the century and in 1869 William and Edward Hodgson were joint lords of the manors.

By 1878, the Hodgson's had been replaced by William Benson Richardson and Henry Cowling, but in 1890 were still listed as being principal land owners along with John Hodgson, Alfred Walker, Francis Theakstone, J. F. Bairstow, W. S. Hornby, John Illingworth, Mrs. Briskham, J. L. Pexton and James Melrose.

THE CHURCH

Information about the date when a church first existed in Haxby is conflicting. It is likely that originally services and ceremonies were held in the open, perhaps beneath a cross. The base of an old stone cross still stands in the churchyard and when Robert son of Maldred ceeded his rights in 1227, the boundaries described began with the words, "from the place where the cross stood [in 1167]". Unfortunately this is anything but conclusive since crosses were erected for a number of other reasons.

11

One further scrap of evidence was found as late as 1978 in the garden of 54 The Village, some 100 yards from the present church. It is a sandstone Anglo-Scandinavian cross-shaft, unfortunately in several pieces. Inspection by the Yorkshire Archaeological Society indicated that the stone was not found locally and was probably brought from the Pennines, although the North Yorks Moors was a possible source. The cross-shaft is decorated with interlaced figures of eight, a common motif for such artefacts, and is possibly early tenth century.

In line with the township being split between two manors, the chapel, too, was divided between Driffield and Strensall. Driffield is some eighteen miles from Haxby and was therefore effectively inaccessible to the villagers. Strensall parish church, on the other hand, is a mere two miles away but the area between Haxby and Strensall was subject to flooding by the Foss which meant the inhabitants of Haxby were frequently cut off from that place of worship too.

A worse problem in time of flooding was that the dead of Haxby could not be decently buried. In 1328, the inhabitants petitioned the Dean and Chapter of York for their own burial ground quoting the scandalous occurrence of the loss of Thomas Westiby's body in the Foss when being carried for burial to Strensall in particularly bad conditions. Their petition was successful and the cemetery was duly dedicated on Friday 17th of June of that year.

At that time the church was referred to as a chapel of Driffield and in the same year it is recorded that the chaplain who celebrated the services at Haxby should receive "all the oblations and Quadragesimal tithes" due from the tenants of both prebends. In 1472, the villagers presented another petition requesting their own priest rather than be dependant on Strensall or Driffield. This petition, too, appears to have been granted because the Commissioners surveying chantries in 1546 document the incumbent as being John Ive, whose only income was "the profitts" of St. Mary's. This amounted to a net figure of 57s. 8d. from copihold land belonging to the church.

By the 16th century, St. Mary's was described as the chapel of Our Lady in Strensall parish. This was confirmed by the returns of Archbishop Herring's visitation of the parish in 1743. In these, Haxby was designated a chapel of ease, without a curate, belonging to Strensall parish, and the vicar of Strensall, C. William Pool, held services in the morning at Strensall and in the afternoon at Haxby. To the present generation, brought up on a religious routine of at least a morning and evening service every Sunday, this might seem a little lax. However, when compared with the York city and suburban parishes, and nearby country parishes, it was much better than the norm for the time. In

i   The former Church. This photograph probably dates from the early 1870s: the Church was destroyed by fire in 1878.

ii   The Vicarage, built in 1864. From the costume of the seated figures, this photograph appears to date from the Edwardian era.

13

1764, for most villages surrounding York, services were conducted fortnightly or even monthly and Communion was frequently restricted to Easter, Whitsun, Michaelmas and Christmas.

At the time of enclosure in 1771, the vicar of Strensall, and therefore minister of Haxby, was the Rev. Thomas Moseley; at this time his tithes were commuted by the allocation of five acres of land under the Act. The living also benefited from the rents due from seventy acres of land and six cottages left to the church. The chapel remained subject to Strensall church until 1862 when Haxby was established as a parish in its own right. In 1864, a vicarage was built on Haxby Moor at a cost of £1,700.

The sixteenth century Norman church was demolished in 1878 and now survives only in photographs. There is just a hint that its demolition was the cause of some argument at the time. One newspaper report of the day describes it as "more like a barn than a Temple set aside for the service of Almighty God", and another as delapidated and unfit for divine worship and records that a fund for its restoration had been set up by the Rev. R. Bradley. However the restoration never took place and all arguments became academic when the church was gutted by fire in 1878. Oddly, no mention was made of

iii   *The present Church of St. Mary, built and completed in the same year, 1878.*

14

the fire in the newspaper report covering the decision to replace "the ancient and unsightly fabric with one of elegant proportions". In the same year, working to plans produced by a Mr. Demaine, the present day church was built on the same site at an estimated cost of £1,800. The report described the church as early Gothic in style and able to seat 200 worshippers; Bulmer's directory of 1890 adds the information that it had a chancel, nave, south porch and western tower containing two bells.

In 1911, the nave was extended by three bays to the west which presumably meant the demolition and rebuilding of the tower and a possible reduction from two bells to one. Local people recall the presence of two bells early in the century but by 1914, the VCH entry records that "the single bell bears the inscription 'Fili Dei miserere mei, 1621' ". Later the single bell too was replaced by an electro-mechanical system driven by a keyboard, and a newspaper article of 1965 records that the refurbished "bells" of Haxby had been installed in the Holy Redeemer Church, Acomb. This is confirmed by the booklet for the opening of the church which refers to the two bells from Haxby parish church being recast after fire damage and transferred to the Acomb church.

The VCH also records the plate as predating the present building, comprising "a cup of 1769 (Newcastle), a paten of 1704 (London), and a modern flagon (London, 1877)". The registers date from the seventeenth century and could be an important source of information for many aspects of village life and history over the last three centuries.

CHARITIES

Like every other parish in the 18th and 19th centuries, Haxby had its poor and, for part of the time at least, was responsible for the administration of the Poor Law for those who qualified. In 1786, the Haxby vestry took steps to ensure that the migrant element of the population did not drift towards their village by fining any person who let a house without observing parish rules which required the presentation of "a leagal certificate". However, Haxby was not without its benefactors and the Poor Law payments were supplemented by charities set up by local people and recorded in the Charity Commissions report of 1876.

In 1733, the Rev. Bayley purchased about 1 acre of land for £20 (Poor's Close), for the purpose of funding a charity. The land was rented out in small gardens and the £3 6s. annual revenue raised was distributed among the poor of the village. An unknown donor left £3 1s. per annum for the same purpose. In 1831, at a time when agriculture nationally was passing through one of its worst depressions, a Mr. Edmonson bequeathed the interest of a deposit of £5 (in 1876 this was 3s per annum), to be distributed in the same way. In 1863, Thomas Thompson gave £10, the interest on which (6s.) was to be used for educational purposes, and a further £100 of North Eastern Railways debentures, the dividends from which were to be distributed to poor widows.

Members of the Hodgson family, which was of some influence in the village at this time, also made bequests. In 1891, John Hodgson left York Corporation stock worth £150, the dividends of which (£4 10s.) were to be used to buy articles for the poor, while a year later, William Hodgson left £500 of the same stock, directing that half of the dividends should be distributed among the poor and the other half used for church purposes. The total dividend in this case was £15.

Other endowments by Lady Henley and the Methodist Chapel are mentioned but not detailed in the report.

ROMAN CATHOLIC RECUSANTS

It appears that the Roman Catholic movement was never strong in Haxby until the influx of new inhabitants in recent years. In fact, they had to wait for a church of their own until 1984, although for some years before that, in an example of the religious cooperation of the times, they held services in St. Mary's. Their modern church is named after the youthful St. Margaret Clitherow who was martyred in 1586 in York for holding to her faith in a time of persecution.

Records of recusants during the 16th century indicate that the Wapentake of Bulmer had a relatively large number of Catholics who refused to bend to the considerable pressures of the time. Some eighty-five names are listed, including fifteen in Huntington, seven in Sutton on Forest, and five in Strensall. In Haxby itself, however, the records show only two families in 1580, one individual in 1590, one in 1604 and none from 1706 to 1780. Archbishop Herring's report in 1743 states that there were neither dissenters nor meeting hall in the parish. Wigginton records one recusant in 1595, one in 1716 and between 1735 and 1743, none in 1764-5 and one in 1780.

One interesting Haxby personage to emerge from the records of the time is Elizabeth Elmhirst. She was the second wife of Richard Elmhirst of Houndhill who predeceased her, and the daughter of Thomas Wayte of Haxby. In her will in 1657, Elizabeth left her various belongings to her four daughters Anne, Ellen, Elizabeth and Mary, and her son Richard. Also "To the poor of Worsbrough, Barnsley and Haxbie, 30s. at the descretion of cousins Robt Allot and Geo. Wilkinson and brother Byrie". Her executors were her uncle John Agar and his son John, her brother Thos Wayte, John Astell, Wm. Faireby and cousin Edward Gaile.

This will offers a wealth of names of substantial families of the time and three further documents both widen the circle and supply more details. The first occurs in 1646, in the records of the Committee for Compounding with Delinquents. This grand sounding organisation was simply a means of Parliament raising funds to support its army in Scotland, by penalising former supporters of the king. The committee accused Richard Elmhirst of fortifying his house as a garrison for the king and his estates were sequentered as a recusant. Although Elizabeth is not definitely recorded as a catholic, it is possible that she was and perhaps that the Wayte family, although traditionally important members of the congregation of St. Mary's, were sympathetic to the recusants' cause.

The second document is the 1653 will of Thomas Driffeild (sic) of Haxby, Gent. Driffeild required that he be buried in the chapel of Haxby and that all his lands in the open common of Easingwold should be sold for payment of debts and for taking care of his younger children. The residue of his lands in Easingwold, Husthwaite, etc., he gave to his son and heir William. His executors form an interesting list of names when compared with Elizabeth Elmhirst's will; they were Thomas Waite of Stillington and John Agar of Stockton. A third executor is a William Laxenbie of Haxby.

The final piece in the jig-saw is again from the proceedings of the Committee for Compounding with Delinquents. In 1654 they record a successful petition by a William Lazenby of Haxby asking that sequestered lands of Mary Willy in Ugthorpe should be released to him because of her death. Given the vagueries of spelling of the time and the links with recusants, it seems possible that Lazenby and Laxenbie are one and the same, in which case a further link in the chain of Roman Catholic families and sympathisers would be established.

NON-CONFORMISTS

In the eighteenth century the non-conformist movement began to emerge in Haxby; a subject dealt with in detail by Ian Winduss in *The story of Methodism in Haxby and Wigginton*. Methodism first arrived in 1777 and the first chapel was created in 1782 in North Lane. The movement flourished and in 1813 a larger chapel was built in the

iv   The former Wesleyan Chapel, constructed in 1813.

main street. This too was abandoned as too small in 1879 and is now privately owned and used as the village fish and chip shop. Apart from the lower storey facia, however, the building remains largely unchanged and its proportions and size are still recognisable as typical of nineteenth century Methodist chapels. The present day chapel was built in 1879 almost on the parish boundary with Wigginton at an estimated cost of £1,342.

In 1829, John Lyth of York had Eastfield House built in Haxby and moved into the village. This was one of the few dwellings in the parish on the Haxby to York road and remained there until 1984 when it was demolished to make room for a small estate of private houses. Lyth was an ardent Methodist and held weekly prayer meetings in Eastfield House.

Primitive Methodism arrived in the village in 1834 and eventually a chapel was built at the junction of the main street and Westfield Road where it is still to be found today. It is no longer a chapel, however, having done service in its lifetime as an ambulance station and the NRCC buildings maintenance office and is now used by a company called Northern Scientific.

v   *The former Primitive Methodist Chapel, constructed in the second quarter of the nineteenth century.*

EDUCATION

Little information is easily available about education before late in the 19th century, but some idea of literacy levels can be gleaned from analysis of signatures versus "marks" on official documents required to be completed by the general public. For example, in the Haxby marriage registers for 1813 to 1837, 46 marriages are recorded, all the women and 50% of the men being residents of the village. Of the women, 61% signed their names while 39% made a mark; of the men 62% signed as against 38% who made a mark. If the men from other parishes are included, the male percentages become 65% and 35% respectively. In total, signing levels of only 50% before 1820 rose to be 69% by the end of the period. These figures compare very closely with national percentages for the time which show that of 5,443 bridegrooms married between 1815 and 1844, 65% were found to have signed their names. When using this information, however, it should be remembered that the ability of someone to sign his name is not a guarantee of any further writing skill, nor does the making of a mark mean that the person cannot read.

19

vi   The Dame's School.

Dames' schools were one of the earliest forms of elementary education open to the children of the ordinary family. Their name was derived from the fact that they were run by untrained elderly women and it is now believed that they were little more than nursery schools where working women could leave their children for a very small fee. The Newcastle Commission of 1861 reported that "Dames' schools are very common in both the country and in towns", and were "generally very inefficient". Haxby's dame's school was housed in a small building on the village green which still exists. Today it is divided into two cottages known as 65 and 67 The Village. Older inhabitants of the village recall that it became a private school for boarders later in the 19th century.

The position on more formal education in 1743 is recorded as a result of Archbishop Herring's visitation. Herring's returns reported that Haxby had "a Private English School, without solary [salary?] but what arises from the scholars". A dramatic improvement on this apparently very basic establishment is found by 1823, when the Rev. John Heslop founded the Classical and Mathematical Boarding Academy in Haxby Hall under the supervision of Matthias Millington.

vii   *The Memorial Hall, built as the village school in 1876, seen (above) after extension in 1903, and (below) in its present modified form.*

An impressive curriculum was published in 1835 when a Mr. Storey advertised the re-opening of what was now his academy. As well as Latin, Greek, French, English literature and composition, history, geography and all branches of mathematics, it included surveying, engineering, navigation and astronomy, and even map drawing "according to the various dimensions of the sphere". The academy was advertised for the sons of "Gentlemen of high respectability".

According to a map of 1851, the village school for the ordinary child was located in South Lane, behind the site of the present day Haxby Shopping Centre. At some time between then and 1875, the school moved to a building in North Lane which is now known as St. Mary's Hall. In 1875 a School Board of five members was set up and a year later the village built a new school at a cost of £2,200. By 1890, it housed over 100 pupils and was in the care of a schoolmaster called Jonathan Arnold. The village was growing more rapidly now, however, and in 1903, under the headmastership of Mr. Marshall, the school was extended to include a new infants department and the accommodation increased to cope with 212 pupils. The 1876 building served as a school until 1954 when it was superceded by the Ralph Butterfield County Primary School on Station Road, it was then converted into the village memorial hall, dedicated to the fallen of both world wars and is used for many community activities. The population explosion in the village since 1970 has required two further schools, one on Oaken Grove and another, Headlands School, on Oaktree Lane.

CHAPTER III

The 18th and 19th Centuries

By the early 18th century, Haxby must have displayed all the features of the classic Vale of York street-village. It comprised two rows of farms and dwelling houses facing each other across a wide main track, with each row serviced by a back lane. The township lay virtually in the centre of four arable fields with a large area of common grazing land to the north of the parish and what was probably a natural water meadow to the east. Until 1769, farming was based on the open field system with people owning various strips in the four main fields and sharing rights to the common grazing land. Map B shows the likely boundaries of the six open fields.

ENCLOSURE

Gradually, the movement to tame and exploit the land won from the forest gathered pace and in 1769 the landowners of Haxby combined to enclose and re-allot the common fields by an act of parliament. In the Act the field names and approximate sizes are given as follows: York Field, 70 acres; Mill Field, 90 acres; Whiteland Field, 107 acres; North Field or Lund Field, otherwise called the Setcop Field and Lund Field, 74 acres; Haxby Common, 1,300 acres; Low Field, 25 acres. The Act records the reasons given by the landowners for enclosing as "the said several open arable Fields and Moor or Common might be greatly improved, if the same were inclosed and divided into specifick Allotments amongst the several Parties interested therein".

One particular clause in the Act gives the trustees powers to transform the medieval landscape into the village we know today. In it they are charged to lay out the public roads which "shall not be less Breadth than Sixty Feet between the Ditches", and to appoint all private roads and ways, fences, drains, ditches, bridges, gates, stiles, causeways,

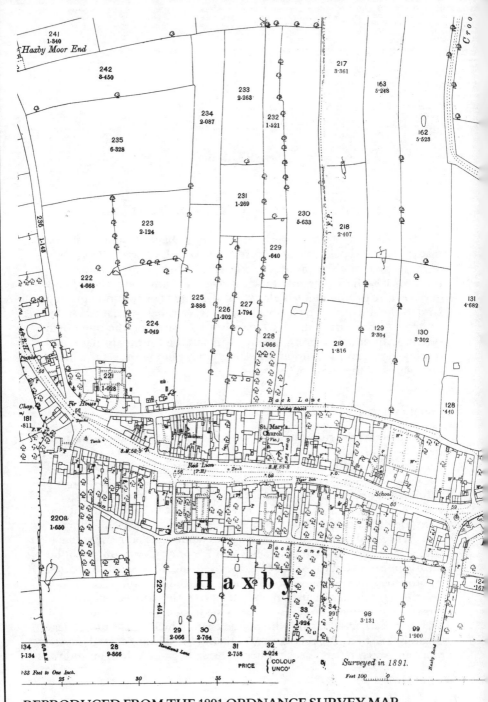

REPRODUCED FROM THE 1891 ORDNANCE SURVEY MAP

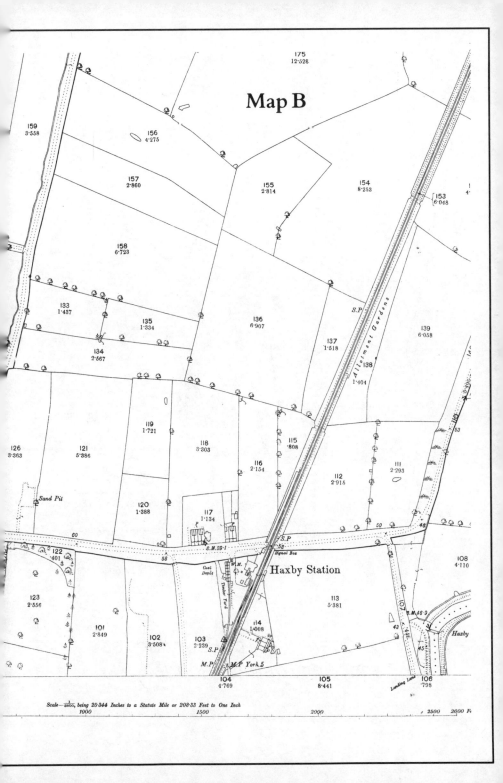

Map B

175
12·528

159
3·558

156
4·275

157
2·860

155
2·814

154
8·253

153
6·048

158
6·723

133
1·437

135
1·334

136
6·907

137
1·518

139
6·058

134
2·567

138
1·404

S.P.

119
1·721

118
3·303

115
·808

126
3·363

121
5·386

116
2·154

112
2·915

111
2·293

Sand Pit

120
1·388

117
1·134

60

B.M.59·1

S.P.

Signal Box

122
·401

58

B.M.59·1

Coal Depôt

W.M.

Haxby Station

108
4·110

123
2·556

113
5·381

B.M.46·9

101
2·849

102
3·508

103
2·239

114
1·008

43

Haxby

S.P.

M.P.

M.P. York 5

104
4·769

105
8·441

106
·798

Landing Lane

Allotment Gardens

Timber Yard

Scale—1/2500, being 25·344 Inches to a Statute Mile or 208·33 Feet to One Inch

1000   1500   2000   2500   2600 Fe

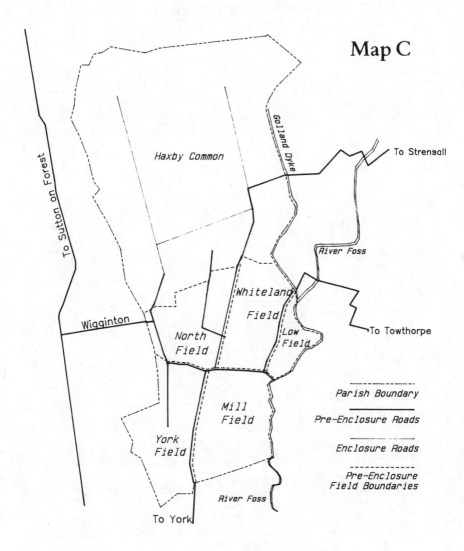

Map C

To Strensall

Golland Dyke

Haxby Common

River Foss

To Sutton on Forest

Whiteland Field

Wigginton

North Field

Low Field

To Towthorpe

Mill Field

------------ Parish Boundary

―――――――― Pre-Enclosure Roads

_____ Enclosure Roads

- - - - - - - Pre-Enclosure Field Boundaries

York Field

River Foss

To York

Haxby Open Field Boundaries and Enclosure Roads

26

watercourses, banks and sluices. In other words, all the features which determine the nature and character of the land. In addition, they could divert the course of water wherever they thought appropriate. One result is the present day combination of old and new roads. On the one hand, we have the road which winds through Wigginton and Haxby then on to Towthorpe, following the lines of the old English/Viking fields; on the other we have the long, straight roads north of the village, laid down by the commissioners of the Act. The latter either stop dead at the boundaries of the enclosed area or dwindle away into the older winding lanes to Strensall.

Some insight into the sort of livestock in the village is gleaned from the clause warning the inhabitants of the penalty for letting their animals damage the newly planted hedges. Those mentioned are "sheep, horses, asses, beasts or other cattle". One surprising ommission is any mention of pigs.

The Haxby enclosure appears to have been an unusually democratic arrangement, no fewer than sixty-five proprietors receiving allotments of land. By comparison, its neighbour Wigginton had only thirty allotees and Skelton a mere nine. Under the Act, all ancient tithes and charges were commuted into land ownership and old enclosures were taken into account. The ancient rights of both lords of the manors and the church were settled by the allotment of portions of land before the other allotments were made. In all, their portion amounted to two-fifteenths of the total enclosure. The award document is in fairly poor condition but names all the allotees and their acreage; the allotment map, an extremely valuable document to a local historian, unfortunately has been lost.

The commissioners appointed to execute the Act were John Graves and John Lund, Gentlemen, of York, and John Outram, Gentleman, of Agnes Burton. This they duly did by 1771.

THE FOSS NAVIGATION SCHEME

As early as 1725, ideas about making the Foss navigable had been mooted but it was not until 1770 that a meeting of the land-owners bordering the Foss as far north as Sheriff Hutton considered a plan. Presumably the newly allotted inhabitants of Haxby were present or at least representatives of the lords of the manors. However, it was not until 1791 that a definite project was set in hand. A group meeting to discuss ways of controlling the perennial problem of the Foss flooding, decided on a navigation scheme from York to Sheriff Hutton.

Although primarily to improve drainage, the plan included the intention to carry coal and road materials on the river. A fascinating record of the history of the canal's development is to be found in *Canals of Yorkshire and North East England* and in *The River Foss — its History and Natural History*.

A well known canal engineer called William Jessop was engaged to do the survey and his estimated cost of the project was £16,274. The narrow, winding and sluggish Foss was to be widened and controlled by locks and one result would be to release some 70 acres of land beneath the walls of York from constant flooding "which in summer is in a putrid state", and turn it "into a rich and verdant mead". Jessop also felt that a reasonably profitable trade on the navigation would be probable.

In 1792, in response to a request from Stephen Croft and Francis Chomley, the group agreed to extend the plan to reach Stillington and an act of parliament in 1793 empowered them to begin. The company had two solicitors, one of whom was named John Lund. Lund was experienced in the problems of drainage and navigation from his time as commissioner to build the Market Weighton canal. It is possible that this is the same man who was a commissioner of the Haxby enclosure act, but, since the name was a common one at the time, it is by no means certain.

Work began in 1793 under the supervision of John Moon but bad management and a failure to follow Jessop's plans, meant the project ran into trouble. By 1795, the navigation was open from York to Haxby but Moon was overspending and was dismissed to be replaced by William Scruton. The main traffic was in coal and lime upstream and grain, butter, bacon, timber and stone downstream.

The shareholders were unhappy about progress and had to be forced by a further act of parliament in 1800 to subscribe the outstanding capital on their shares to continue the work as far as Sheriff Hutton bridge. In 1802 enough money had been gathered to go ahead. A long cut was made from a point just east of Strensall to avoid a sweeping bend in the narrowing river and this terminated at canal head, close to the juncture of the Stillington road with the Strensall to Sheriff Hutton road. The stage was completed by mid 1804 at which point the navigation was 11.5 miles long and had cost about £35,000.

The viability of the navigation did not improve and the company tried to abandon the plan to go as far as Stillington but were prevented from doing so by Croft and Sir Charles Harland. Toll revenue was disappointing and calls for extra payments on shares caused disaffection amongst the shareholders. In 1810 the company agreed to continue the project at a cost of £10,000 and a survey was begun; it appears, however, that the work was never undertaken. Today, canal head is an isolated empty ditch with part of the cut at Bridge Farm ploughed over and not even discernible.

The death knell finally sounded for profitable trade on the Foss navigation when the York to Scarborough branch of the York and North Midlands Railway opened in 1845. Map C shows the inter-relation of road, river and rail transport for the area and illustrates how the railway absorbed the traffic for all the villages between York and Strensall including Haxby. Nevertheless, we still have Haxby Landing and Haxby Lock as reminders of the abortive project, but more importantly we have the vastly improved drainage that was the original intention of its instigators.

viii   Lock House, built about 1800, with the weir in the foreground.

THE YORK AND NORTH MIDLANDS RAILWAY

The chairman of the Y. & N.M. was the controversial George Hudson and its engineer was George Stephenson, a formidable combination of entrepreneurial flair and technical ability. The story of the York to Scarborough branch line began with a public meeting in Scarborough Town Hall in 1839 where both men explained their plan. Although it met with support, more important projects took priority with them until 1844 when they finally submitted an Act to Parliament.

The generally flat terrain between York and Scarborough, plus the decision to follow the winding valley of the Derwent rather than tunnel through the Howardian Hills, meant that the forty two miles of line were built in less than a year. In July 1845 it was opened with Hudson's usual flamboyancy. The festivities included a public breakfast in York prior to embarking on the inaugural trip, an equally public lunch on the temporary Scarborough station on arrival there, and a dinner in York Town Hall on their return for a guest list of 700 notables. The full story of the line is covered in *A Regional History of the Railways of Great Britain*.

The line included the construction of housing for the railway staff, Haxby Station and Haxby Gates signal box and introduced a new source of employment into the village. In the census of 1861, the heads of four families, comprising nineteen people, lived in the village and worked for the railway; the station master at that time was a Mr. Eastgate. By 1913, a successor called Mr. Gordon commanded a staff of eleven at what must have been a thriving station. Passenger traffic on the line was brisk; by 1905, the number of people travelling between York and Scarborough had risen to almost 330,000 per annum, producing an income of £48,000. Obviously, some of these must have been from Haxby and the surrounding villages which used Haxby station. In addition, the goods traffic proved to be highly profitable, the receipts generated in 1905 amounting to almost £10,000 and derived from handling "parcels, horses, carriages and dogs". The area was without coal, the most prevalent fuel of the time, and the railway transported substantial quantities of this and argicultural produce at the expense of the Foss navigation and the local carters. The OS map for 1891 shows a large coal depot located close to Haxby station.

Along with many others, the station was closed in the 1960s and the platforms demolished. The stationmaster's house still exists, however, as does the signalman's house at Haxby Gates, although, at the time of writing, signal box and signalman's house are under threat of demolition in favour of a wider, automated barrier. The line itself is still part of the national rail network with routine services on it and now boasts summertime steam excusions from York to Scarborough. In recent years, suggestions have been made that the stations at Haxby and Strensall should reopen to ease the continually worsening peak hour road traffic problems.

Map D

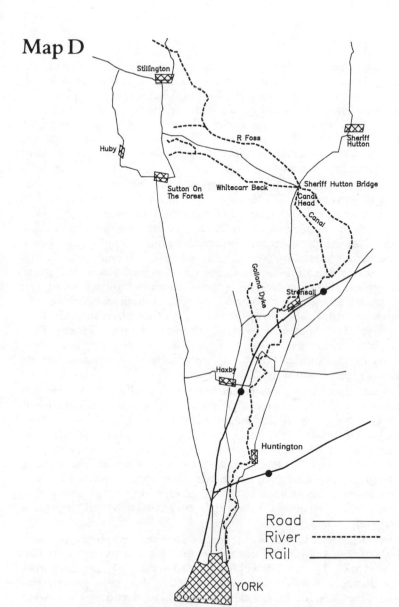

Stillington

Sheriff
Hutton

Huby

R Foss

Sutton On
The Forest

Whitecarr Beck

Sheriff Hutton Bridge

Canal
Head

Canal

Golland Dyke

Strensall

Haxby

Huntington

Road ———
River --------
Rail ━━━━━

YORK

Road, River and Rail Transport
Mid 19th Century

OCCUPATIONS

Farming and ancillary businesses were the main industry throughout the period and this is illustrated by analysis of occupations listed in the national census returns of the time. In 1801, 73 adults were employed in agriculture while 21 carried on other occupations. In 1831, of the 92 males over twenty years of age in the village, 63 were either farmers or farm labourers while 29 were employed otherwise. By 1861, the family heads who were either farmers or their employees numbered 89, with 47 being employed in other occupations.

Two major changes occurred between the Enclosure Act and the end of the 19th century. In 1769, awards of land were made to sixty-five people; by 1861, there were only 38 farmers in the census and in 1890, a directory of the village listed only 28 farmers and named no more than 14 farms. Nevertheless, farming remained the major employer well into the present century. The second interesting fact to emerge from the 1861 census is that none of the farmers at that time was a local man. Although the majority were from the surrounding townships, others had come from Bridlington, North Cave and Durham and even from as far afield as Suffolk and Shropshire. On the other hand, about 50% of the agricultural labourers working for them were born in Haxby. This raises two questions. Why had the farms changed hands so dramatically? Why did not the local men involved in agriculture buy up the farms as they became available?

In addition to large-scale agriculture, the village had a market gardening industry and in 1890 William Carr and Joseph Clarke are listed as proprietors in that business. Most villages had a resident blacksmith to maintain the farming equipment but Haxby boasted two blacksmiths in 1861 and there was still employment for two, although different men, in 1890. Other ancillary trades were joiner, wheelwright and thrashing machine proprietor, while supporting businesses were dealers in straw, hay, potatoes and timber. One business extant in 1861, the name of which at least lasted right into the 1980s, was Boynton's joinery shop.

In 1801, the official census recorded 21 people employed in trade, manufacturing and handicrafts and by the 1861 census the figure had increased to 47. The sort of people included in the 1861 categories were the landlords of the Red Lion and Tiger Inn, butchers, grocers and greengrocers, dressmakers, shoemakers and launderesses. There were also the local bailiff, parish clerk, road surveyor, school teachers, constable and post-master. Transport for people and goods was available from a well staffed Haxby station from 1845, but the local carters still existed. In 1890 William Hodgson of Ivy Cottage advertised as "carrier to York, on Mondays, Fridays and Saturdays". Haxby also contained people who described themselves as "gentlemen", "annuity holders", "landed proprietors", etc. and there were, of course, the local JP and lords of both manors. In fact all the elements were present that indicated a thriving, self supporting and self-managing village life.

One not so traditional job was that of Mrs. Frances Ann Thompson. In 1890, she is listed as a farmer "and hobby horse, etc., prioprietor". The same lady was still operating her sideshows around the local village feasts well into the present century.

BRICK AND TILE MAKING

One of the reasons for Haxby's constant battle against flooding was the thick seam of clay which underlies the fertile top-soil; its presence, however, had its positive side in that it gave rise to the manufacture of bricks and tiles. The clay was dug from two large pits and baked in a firing house which still stands on the premises. Some of the local houses built in the latter part of the 19th century are constructed of Haxby bricks and tiles and the author of the 1976 conservation order attributes the common use of those materials in the village to the presence of the brickyards.

Perhaps the most notable person to be involved with the industry was Thomas Holtby. Holtby was a stage coach driver in the first half of the 19th century and was noted for his dash and style in driving. When the days of the coaches were ended by the new railways, he opened up as a horse-breaker in York and about 1833, he moved to Haxby and took over the brickyard in York Road. He apparently had considerable personal charisma but it does not seem to have been matched by his business acumen. The brickyard venture failed and Holtby also lost a reputed £600 as part owner of a newspaper and £800 through his involvement with the Agicultural bank as well as other, smaller sums. Nevertheless, when he was finally laid to rest in Haxby churchyard in 1863, he was still worth over £3,000.

By 1851, Holtby had shed the brickyard business to the Driffield family from Terrington. The census of that year lists Henry, Francis and George Driffield as brick and tile manufacturers, with each supporting a burgeoning family. The name of Driffield became synonymous with brickmaking for many years in Haxby and it is therefore surprising that, in the trade directory for 1890, a Mrs. Elizabeth Bulmer alone is recorded as a brickmaker. By 1911, however, a report in the Yorkshire

Gazette records that "the old industry of brick-making, whose former prosperity is indicated by several decayed miniature windmills (formerly used for pumping purposes) along the York Road, has almost gone".

The two large pits are now flooded and have become a nature reserve, given over to wild life and fishing. However, two of the small pumping houses which controlled the water when the quarries were in use still exist, one of them having been fully restored.

CHAPTER IV

Haxby in the Twentieth Century

The character of Haxby has undergone more change in the twentieth century than in the nine which preceeded it. In the span of one lifetime, it has changed from a rural village with agriculture as the dominant employment, to a dormitory suburb for York workers. It therefore seems most appropriate to chronicle the changes as seen through the eyes of someone who experienced them first hand. Haxby is fortunate enough to have an excellent short memoir of the period between 1902-1974, written by a lady whose recollections are at once objective and personal. They are reproduced here with explanatory information, where necessary, added in square brackets.

"MEMORIES OF HAXBY, 1902-1974"

On August 19th 1902, I came with my parents and two brothers and a baby sister to live in Haxby. The village at that time only extended from Usher Lane corner to the Methodist Chapel and was mainly occupied by farmers. What is now North Lane was then known as the Back Lane and the residents lived in the small terrace houses and generally worked on the farms or other occupations in the village.

The terrace of houses on York Road near the village had been recently built as had a few houses near the railway station. There was a useful train service and a number of railway people had to live in the village and quite a lot of children went into York to school. The train fare was 4d. single and 7d. return. Many folks used to walk one way.

The village school, built in 1876 had replaced a previous schoolroom behind the Church, (now St. Mary's Hall). The schoolmaster was Mr. Marshall who lived with his family in the adjoining schoolhouse. He was assisted by an uncertificated teacher named Miss Jefferson and Mrs. Marshall used to come in to superintend the girls sewing lessons. The school consisted of two rooms facing the village street and the scholars sat in fixed desks, each seating 5 or 6 scholars. There were no backs to the seats and just a small shelf under the desk itself for books. Later another classroom and boys and girls cloakrooms were built behind as the village was growing and an extra infants teacher was appointed named Miss Bull.

In addition to the Railway service there was a carriers cart owned by Mr. W. Hodgson who took passengers and goods into York each Saturday and brought others back. He could take about 6 adult passengers in his covered cart drawn by a farm horse and I believe the fare was 6d. and the journey took 1 hour.

There was no tarmac in those days and the roads were quite rough with cobbles and potholes and so very muddy. Each Saturday one of the roadmen, Mr. Johnson, used to scrape the road in the village with a wide wheeled scraper which he dragged across, gathering the mud into heaps at the side of the road. The footpaths were quite attractive. They were covered with boiler ashes which at that time could be obtained free for carting from Rowntrees. They were a red brick colour and grass grew like a kerb at the road side. In general the paths were nice and firm but after frosty weather they became very sticky.

There were no street lights except at the station where paraffin lamps were lit to show the way in and out of the trains. Indoor lighting was by means of oil lamps too until 1912 and 1913 when gas and electricity were brought to the village. York water had been extended into the village about 1907-08, but it was some time before all the houses were connected.

The village folks tended to stay near home for their work and several farming families worked on their land without extra help. There were the Brittons, Jeffersons, Harpers, Abel, Marriott, Hopkinson and Scotts.

[Other businesses listed by the author are:]
Builders, Boyntons; Blacksmith, Atkinson; Tailor, Falkingham; Dressmakers, Mrs. Hall, Miss Cornforth; Shopkeepers, J. W. Bentley, Miss Jefferson, Miss Braithwaite, Co-op Stores; Newsagents, Jorville; Post office, Mr. and Mrs. Wintle; Butcher, Mr. Eglin; Shoe-mender, J. A. Johnson; Postman, Noble.

Haxby Hall was a pleasant Georgian property at the junction of York Road, Station Road and the village street, with extensive gardens and parkland and occupied by Mr. W. Wood and family. This has now been demolished and the old people's home, (also called Haxby Hall) built on the site. The gardener's cottage stood where the ambulance station is now.

An annual event was Haxby Feast, when a shooting gallery and rowing boats with one or two stalls for sweets and oddments were set up outside the Red Lion Inn. These shows were the property of a village resident, Mrs. Fanny Thompson, who lived with her family by the present fish shop [No. 53 The Village] and in the summer she used to travel around the villages with her show. There was also the Haxby Agricultural and Horticultural Society Show which was usually held on the last Wednesday in July, a great day for everyone.

The village clock on the Memorial Hall (formerly the village school), was put there to commemorate the coronation of King Edward VII in 1902 (there is a crown on the top of the clock still), and I believe the tree on the roundabout was planted for the Jubilee of Queen Victoria in 1897. In 1911 we celebrated the Coronation of King George V, with a tea for everyone in a barn and sports on the cricket field in Headlands Lane. The copper beech tree on the Green was planted to celebrate the event. For King George VI coronation seats were provided on the village green, Station Road and York Road and for Queen Elizabeth we planted trees and shrubs on the village green and verges but unfortunately only one shrub near Church House remains.

The Memorial Hall is the successor to a smaller one in South Lane. This was originally a barn which was converted as a social meeting place for the village after the 1914–1918 war, largely due to the initiative of the Mason family who lived at Eastfield House, and served for many years until the land was sold for building and the old school became available and offered more room.

St. Mary's Church and the Wesleyan Methodist Chapel have played a continuing part in the life of the village. In the early days there was also a Primitive Methodist Chapel which closed when amalgamated with the Wesleyan Methodists. It became an ambulance station and during the 1939–1945 war the air raid siren was stationed there. It is now used by the N.R.C.C. [Now Northern Scientific].

St. Mary's Church was originally linked with Strensall and was served from there. In order to warn parishioners that there would be a service the bells rung for about ten minutes at 1 hour before the service time: 9.30 for 10.30 service. There were two bells rung for 10 minutes and one bell for 5 minutes. The present building replaced an earlier one which was destroyed by fire. The font at the west end was in the old church and after a considerable time was found in the garden at the Hall and restored to the church. When it was rebuilt the building only extended as far as the South door but was enlarged westwards in 1911 and a new vestry added in 1921. The pews in the extension were given by parishioners, mainly as memorials.

The Methodist chapel was built in 1879. In days gone by there was a certain rivalry between church and chapel but now there is a much closer communication between the congregations with co-operation for the benefit of the community as much as possible especially among the young folks.

The 1914–1918 war brought changes here as elsewhere. I remember the horses being commandeered and as there were very few motors about then this made for a difficult situation and of course most of the young men went away into the Forces. By 1916 food supplies were getting scarce yet there was no official rationing so it was a case of watching out for the arrival of a cart bringing supplies to a shop and getting out a bike to be there as it was unloaded and even then not being sure of getting what one wanted. In July 1919 the village celebrated the signing of the Peace Treaty with a tea for everyone in the school.

After the end of the war there was an increase in population owing to new houses being built at Park Estate, Southlands and other parts.

There were two brick yards in the Parish, one on York Road where Mr. Driffield had worked for a very long time making bricks and draining tiles. It was a lovely place for youngsters to play in winter when the kilns happened to be empty but were still beautifully warm from the previous firing. The ponds where the clay had been taken out were popular with fishermen as I believe they are still and in a hard winter were thronged with skaters. The other brickyard was in Towthorpe Road and belonged to Mr. Ellis. It was not nearly such a big affair and eventually was used as a refuse tip and the land was built upon.

There was a lot of "Do it yourself" in those days and when the question of a War Memorial for the village was discussed a barn in South Lane was converted into a Social Hall for the village mainly by voluntary labour. The field where the barn stood became a playing field with tennis courts and football pitch, the cricket club already had the use of a field in Headlands Lane. Many were the happy times we spent there with Whist Drives and other social events until the time came for the move to the old school where there was more room for the needs of the growing village.

With the outbreak of the 1939–45 war we had our share of receiving evacuees from Hull and Middlesborough. Haxby Hall became a First Aid Centre and later we had Airmen billeted with us. The Women's Institute members organised a jam making centre where sugar was made available for using surplus fruit. This had to be sold to the shops to help out the rations. We made 500 lbs. in 1941.

After the war the village grew still larger, especially with the building of Council Houses in Calf Close and Usher Lane. The Ralph

Butterfield School was built in Station Road and later the Annex in Usher Lane.

On June 2nd 1953 we celebrated the Coronation of H. M. Queen Elizabeth II, a bitterly cold day with heavy showers but as always the show had to go on. For some months regular collections had been made to defray expenses and preparations made for 2,000 people to have a sit down tea. Two large marquees had been erected on the playing fields which by that time had been given to the village by Mr. Kenneth Ward in memory of his wife. The sports which should have followed had to be postponed for a better day.

Another Royal occasion was the wedding of H.R.H. The Duke of Kent to Miss Katherine Worsley at York Minster when the Bridal Party and all the guests came through Haxby on the way to Hovingham for the reception. It was a glorious sight and everyone had a front view with no crowds. We have also had the Duchess again last year when she came to open "Hanover Court", a development of flats built in North Lane for elderly residents.

The village grows and grows and we miss many old friends but the newcomers are very friendly and we hope they find the old residents equally so.

[Sadly, the author of these memoirs is one of the many old friends that the village now misses.]

LOCAL CUSTOMS AND FOLK LORE

In addition to the feast and horticultural show, there were two other annual events of note at the turn of the century not mentioned in the memoirs, and of course, no history would be complete withou a local ghost.

THE HAXBY SWORD DANCE

In the North Riding, villages such as Kirkby Malzeard, Escrick, Handsworth and Sleights had their Morris Dances and Haxby was no exception. The dancing seemed to be based on competition with our neighbours in Wigginton and might have been a less dangerous combat than the battles which are said to have taken place between the Haxby Terriers and the Wigginton Bulldogs as the youths of the villages dubbed themselves. The dance last took place in about 1890 and each village was represented by a team of fifteen young men. The eight sword dancers were accompanied by an accordian player and light

39

relief was supplied by a Fool, a Besom–Betty, and a King and Queen. Two collectors went among the spectators gathering contributions.

The dancer's costume was a white shirt, black trousers with a red stripe down the seam, and a red cap. The shirts were covered in coloured bows and rosettes and the costume was completed by a white sash over the right shoulder. Each carried a three foot sword of ash. There were nine figures in the dance called The Clash, The Snake, Single–over, Single–under, Double–over, Double–under, Right Shoulder Lock, The Wheel and The Rose. Details of each figure and the music used are available so perhaps we will see the dance revived by the village schools at some future date.

THE PLOUGH STOTT'S PLAY

As recently as March 1987, a further, virtually forgotten custom came to light. An item in the parish magazine reported the first performance since 1922 of a mummers play. This was previously performed every year by the plough apprentices (stotts) of the village. The play had been reconstructed from the recollections of a villager and performed by the local Boy Scouts.

Its story is a traditional allegory of the death of St. George (summer) at the hands of the Killer (winter) and his revival by the Doctor (spring). The Haxby version seems to be unique in that St. George was replaced by King William, but which William is not known.

THE HAXBY GHOST

During the middle ages Haxby could claim a share in the horrific mounted phantom of the Forest of Galtres known as le Gros Veneur (the Big Hunter), who rode around on foul, dark nights and terrified the patrolling foresters. However, an occurrence on just such a night during the "black-out" of the 1939-45 war, gave the village a claim to its very own ghost. John McJarrett, a Highlander by birth, was driving his post van towards York when he spotted the figure of a very old clergyman in the dark and driving rain. He stopped and offered the old man a lift, commenting, "You're a very old man to be out on a wet night like this". "Yes, I was eighty," replied the old clergyman as he got out at the vicarage gates. "Was" was the operative word. McJarrett later discovered that his passenger had died six months earlier!

CHAPTER V

Contemporary Haxby

POPULATION GROWTH

As the author of our memoir above observed in 1974, "the village grows and grows", and that growth has accelerated rather than abated since then. Very tentative estimates of early population can be made from some of the documents already quoted above. For example, Domesday says that there were seven villagers, or land-owning peasants. If we assume that they were all heads of families averaging six people, and add a small number for other classes of inhabitant not recorded, we have a population size of about 50. If we apply the same principle to the Lay Subsidy roll of 1300,we have twenty-four tax payers and a calculated population of about 150. The 1377 Poll Tax gives a figure of 167 people of 14 years and over for Haxby and Wigginton combined, despite two years of famine and three epidemics of plague in the intervening years. Historians suggest that 50% is added for infants between 5 and 25% for those evading tax for some reason. This would give a figure of about 300 for the combined townships.

Between then and the beginning of official census figures we have no easily available data and the first census of 1801 shows a surprisingly small increase in over 400 years to no more than 325 inhabitants. The growth from then until 1970 remained modest but the dramatic change after that date is clear from the following tables.

Table 1. Nineteenth Century

Year	1801	1811	1821	1831	1841	1851	1861	1871	1881	1891	1901
Pop.	325	395	417	412	437	527	597	603	559	619	711

Table 2. Twentieth Century

Year	1901	1911	1921	1931	1941	1951	1961	1971	1981
Pop.	711	833	949	1268	*	2152	2407	3783	9064

*No census figures taken in war-time.

Between 1801 and 1921, growth averaged just over 50 people per decade and the population actually declined marginally in the third decade of the nineteenth century and by 7% in the eighth decade. In fact, in the thirty years between 1861 and 1891, the population grew by only 22 people due mainly to the drift of the surrounding rural population into York. Between 1921 and 1961, growth accelerated to an average of 365 per decade. Thereafter, the figures show two successive and increasing leaps of 1,376 by 1971 and a massive 5,281 by 1981.

Map E shows the correlation between the population increases and the development of the estates which house the additional population. Prior to 1851 there was no discernable development outside the village centre apart from Eastfield House and the railway stationmaster's and signalman's houses. Between 1891 and 1925, there had been some development on the north side of Station Road, along the west side of York Road close to the roundabout, and the small Park Estate had been built.

By 1954, more houses had been built on both sides of Station Road and the east side of Towthorpe Road, and the Calf Close council estate was in place. Apart from Haxby Hall's park-land and a small area north and south of Eastfield House, the whole of York Road was lined with dwellings of various sorts and Hilbra Avenue and Westfield Avenue had been built in the south east corner of York Fields. To the north of the village there had been small developments at Albermarle Gardens and off North Lane and Usher Lane.

By 1966, small estates had been built on three plots off South Lane, including the old orchards and playing fields; the Ralph Butterfield School had appeared on Station Road, and the Windmill Way estate was completed on fields between Usher Lane and the Railway line. On the south side of Station Road, Haxby Hall had been replaced by the old people's home, and Hall Rise and the library had been built. Finally, there had been some strip development on the west side of Towthorpe Road.

The last minor development took place between 1966 and 1974. By this time, the Usher Lane Annex school and its surrounding estate had

42

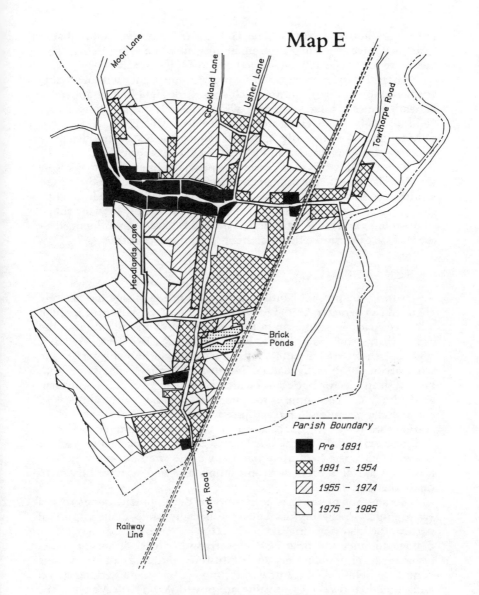

Map E

Moor Lane

Crookland Lane

Usher Lane

Towthorpe Road

Headlands Lane

Brick
Ponds

Parent Boundary

Parish Boundary

Pre 1891

1891 – 1954

1955 – 1974

1975 – 1985

York Road

Railway
Line

Transfer of Land from
Agriculture to Housing

43

been built between North Lane and Usher Lane. Off South Lane, Ableton Grove had filled the remaining gap while Old Orchard had been extended as far as what was to become Holly Tree Lane.

After 1974 the massive building programme began. Within 6 years, virtually the whole of the pre-enclosure York Field had disappeared beneath housing estates together with large areas of Lowfield, Lund Field and Whiteland Field and the whole of Mill Field west of the railway line. Most recently, Eastfield House has been demolished to make way for a small estate and Church Field has been absorbed.

Regrettable as this may be in some ways, it is interesting to see how the boundaries set at the time of enclosure and the even older open field boundaries have been observed during the housing developments. Reference to a sequence of detailed OS maps will show how the shape of the estates and the positioning of the roads have been influenced by the customs, decisions and agreements of so many centuries ago.

THE CHANGING FACE OF HAXBY

During the present century, the centre of the village has entirely changed its character. Until recent times it consisted of little more than a service road between farm houses, several of them still extant in the 1950s. Farms such as Dixon's, Prospect, Abel's, Britton's, Tindall's, Widd's, Usher's are remembered by relatively youthful villagers, while what are now officially named North and South Lanes were both known simply as the back lanes which gave vehicles access to the farm yards. Now the farm houses that survive are either private houses or commercial premises, and are interspersed with shops and banks. Agriculture has been squeezed out in favour of commerce and trade and now exists only on the outskirts of the parish, particularly to the north. What was a road used mainly by cattle and farm machinery, is now daily as full of cars, buses and shoppers as any busy country town on market day.

To attempt to see it as continuity of development rather than a swamping by "progress" is not easy, especially when, daily, important parts of the historic fabric succumb to the pressure placed on it. Fields delineated since the time of enclosure and before, disappear under housing developments, groups of historic buildings in the village centre are demolished for new shopping precincts and parking space, and individual dwellings of value are pulled down to leave gaps like pulled teeth before being replaced by functional, but sometimes ill-matched, dentures. A close study of the 25 inch to the mile Ordnance Survey map of 1891 illustrates some of the major losses in recent years.

ix   Haxby Hall, demolished in 1960, in a photograph taken in the 1950s.

One notable casualty was the impressive Georgian building, Haxby Hall, which formerly stood at the junction of York Road, The Village and Station Road. The Hall was built at the turn of the 18th and 19th centuries and is described in the Yorkshire Gazette in 1853 as having lofty and elegant drawing, dining and sitting rooms, excellent lodging rooms, a double coach-house and stables. The grounds comprised tastefully laid out lawns, large well-stocked gardens, 22 acres of parkland surrounded by ornamental trees, and a fish pond.

The Hall changed hands frequently during its lifetime and it is possible that its upkeep proved too much for some of its owners. Between 1823 and 1835, the Hall was used as an academy for boys, and in 1835 H. Dyson was the owner and tried to sell it by auction in June of that year. It appears he was successful, but in September of the same year a Mr. George Myers put it back on the market for rent. In May 1878, it was put up for sale again by a Mr. Williamson together with an appreciable amount of quality livestock, and a phaeton and dog-cart. The buyer this time, for £4,100, was Alfred Walker of Haxby. In 1890 it was still the property of Alfred Walker and the home of Henry Leetham and by 1914 it was the residence of William Abel Wood, JP. In 1960 it was demolished by the County Council to make way for an old people's home which is an attractive low building, attached to which is the ambulance station. The fish pond no longer exists, and the majority of the old park is now the Ethel Ward memorial playing fields with only a mature line of trees stretching from Hall Rise to the library to remind us of the "pleasure grounds".

In 1984, another substantial building, Eastfield House, which was built for John Lyth 150 years before, was demolished to make way for a small group of private houses. One notable owner was John Kaye,

x   Eastfield House, built in 1829, in a photograph taken shortly before its demolition in 1984.

Alderman of York City Council and one time Lord Mayor of York. All that remains of the original estate are the red brick walls that surrounded the spacious gardens and now enclose the modern dwellings. At the time it was built and for many years afterwards, Eastfield House was the only building between the village and the southern boundary of the parish.

In the centre of the village, Abel's farm and Bell's garage were demolished in 1970 to be replaced by the Haxby Shopping Arcade and in 1986 Leedham's garage and one valuable dwelling were swept away for the even bigger Ryedale Shopping Centre. The former is a typical small late '60s development with little to commend it aesthetically,

46

while the latter has been designed to fit in more with the character and colour of the surrounding architecture.

At the end of 1986, a very interesting house and its attendant outhouses built around a courtyard which comprised No. 43 The Village, were demolished to make way for some sheltered housing. The new building, dubbed in the parish magazine "Carbuncle Court", could hardly be less sympathetic to the character of the main street. Although it complies with the requirements for building materials laid down in the conservation order, it is a massive block of three storeys instead of two, covers the whole site, and dwarfs the buildings on either side in both height and scale. Set between a modern shopping arcade and a Victorian villa, it manages somehow to clash with both, whereas in another setting it would be an attractive structure.

A number of alterations to old property have been less than sympathetic. Perhaps the most extreme cases are the conversion of the fine, spacious methodist chapel, built in 1813, into the village fish and chip shop, and the incongruous replacement of part of the old terrace of cottages at 26/28 The Village by a modern dwelling now housing a grocer's and a butcher's. On the other hand, apart from the latter and the substitution of a sixties style high street bank for what appears on the 1891 map to be a farm and outhouses, the north side of The Village is still very much in tact. The uses to which the property is put have changed to a large extent but much of the fabric of the buildings has been saved, while dwellings such as The Hollies and Wortley House offer an attractive variety of traditional building styles.

Even more encouraging is the survival so far of the groups of 18th or early 19th century dwellings around the green and Wyre Pond at the west end of The Village and the farm buildings near the roundabout at the east end. Other houses on the north side of Station Road and the west side of York Road are rapidly becoming valuable as a records of late 19th and early 20th century architecture. Other individual buildings of value which remain are the vicarage, Grey Firs and the older farms to the north of the village.

All in all, then, there is still a great deal of valuable architecture to be enjoyed and, hopefully, preserved in Haxby, including a number of the old pumps marked on the 1891 map which still exist in courtyards behind the houses.

STREET NAMES

As final proof that history is tenacious and not easily disposed of, some interesting medieval names are perpetuated unexpectedly, and perhaps even unwittingly, in the street names of the very housing estates which threaten to obliterate it. Examples of these are: Eastfield Avenue and Westfield Lane, named after Anglo Saxon open fields; Calf Close, where it is said that cattle were held overnight to safeguard them from theft; Folks Close, which stands on the allotments which used to generate revenue for the poor of the parish; Hall Rise, which is a small cul-de-sac close to the site of the old Haxby Hall.

Perhaps the most poignant of all is Headlands Lane. This continuum of muddy track, occasional patch of tarmac and neglected ancient hedges, forms one of the most historic paths of the parish. The headlands were the stretches of ground between two common fields where ploughmen turned their ploughs perhaps for a millenium. It terminates at the boundary fence of the Headlands School and for that reason ought to be an excellent encouragement of interest in local history for the pupils. Instead, the lane, the name of which has even disappeared from the most recent maps, does not even boast a nameplate.

CONCLUSION

What I set out to do in this short work, was to give a general overview of Haxby's history from the ancient environment which ensured its origins to the influences which have shaped its present. The result has been to trace no more than an outline of a community from the founding Vikings, living off the forest and trading with their Anglo Saxon neighbours, to the dormitory culture of today. I have tried to record how, like so much of Britain, the countryside has been almost hand-crafted by the inhabitants, from the clearing of the land after disafforestation, through the laying of enclosure roads, ditches and hedges, to the improved drainage by means of the Foss navigation scheme and right down to the manicured domestic gardens of the large new estates. The changing face of religious practices and education have been briefly covered and an eye-witness memoir of recent history has been included.

Naturally, there are a number of areas where, given time and access to the records, a great deal more informative detail could be assembled. For example, an analysis of the church registers and wills should fill the massive gap in population statistics as well as giving a human dimension to them. Or again, there must be considerable information available about the development of education in the 18th and 19th centuries which has not been included here. Valuable further projects also suggest themselves, one example being the compilation of a pictorial record of the township, past and present. But perhaps potentially the most rewarding of all, because of the dramatic changes which have occured in Haxby in the last ninety years, would be an oral history project.

I plan to tackle some of these projects in the future, but I would hope that interested readers would not wait for that to happen. Instead I would urge them to research some area of interest to themselves, or publish research they have already done for their own satisfaction. The challenge to wrest information from the archives, or from the village that stands and moves about us day by day, is there to be met. On the other hand, let me suggest on alternative to the solitary study of old documents. Amongst other things, history is a record of life. Is it too late to revive some of the customs and events that brightened the lives of our predecessors? Could such things as the sword dance, the Plough Stotts Play, the horticultural show and the Haxby feast become, once again, annual events, perhaps under the cultural umbrella of the Ryedale festival?

These things will only happen if someones decides to make them.

xi   *A typical Saturday's traffic in today's Haxby. Compare with the cover photograph which dates from the inter-war period.*

49

Bibliography

Awards document of the Enclosure Allotments (1769).
Calenders of Patent Rolls.
Census returns for 1801, 1831, 1851, 1861.
Charity Commissions Report (1876).
Enclosure Act of Parliament 1769.
Proceedings of Courts Baron and Customary Court (1863).
Reports in the Yorkshire Gazette, Yorkshire Herald and York Press.
Victoria County History — North Riding, Vol. II.

H. Aveling	Northern Catholics 1558–1790 (1966)
H. C. Barnard	A History of English Education from 1970 (1963)
T. Bulmer	History and Directory of North Yorkshire (1890)
Mrs. Connings	Memories of Haxby 1902–1974 (ms in private hands)
G. C. Cowling	History of Easingwold and Forest of Galtres (1967)
D. P. Dymond	Writing Local History (1981)
S. Ellis	Placenames in Ryedale: Transactions of Yorkshire Dialect Society (1973)
W. Farrar (editor)	Early Yorkshire Charters (1916)
C. H. Feinstein (ed)	York 1831–1981 (1981)
M. Fife and P. Walls	The River Foss — Its History and Natural History (1973)
T. Gill	Vallis Eboracencis (1852)
C. H. Hadfield	Canals of Yorkshire and North East England (1972)

R. A. Hall (YAJ Vol. 53)	An Anglo-Scandinavian Cross Shaft from Haxby (1981)
B. J. D. Harrison	The 1377 Poll Tax Returns for the North Riding (1970)
R. P. Hastings	Poverty and Poor Law in N. Riding, 1780–1837 (1982)
K. Hoole	A Regional History of the Railways of Gt. Britain Vol. 4 (1965)
G. Lawton	Collectio Rerum Ecclesiasticarum de Diocesi Eboracensi (1840)
John V. Mitchell	Ghosts of an Ancient City (1974)
Cecil J. Sharp	The Sword Dances of Northern England Vol. 3 (1951)
Margaret E. Smith	The Marriage Registers of Haxby 1813–1836 (1979)
Surtees Society records	York Chantries, Guilds, Hospitals, etc. (1895)
Helen M. Turner	The effects of . . . Enclosures . . . of Haxby . . .
P. J. Walls	Haxby Plough Stotts play (The Outlook, March 1987)
L. P. Wenham	Derventia (Malton) (1974)
L. P. Wenham	The Great and Close Seige of York (1970)
G. F. Wilmot et al	York, a Survey 1959 (1959)
Ian Winduss	The story of Methodism in Haxby and Wigginton (1979)
YAS Records Servies Vol. 9	Abstracts of Yorkshire Wills 1665–6 (1890)
YAS Records Series Vols. 15, 20	Royalist Composition Papers (1893, 1896)
YAS Records Series Vol. 31	Yorkshire Inquisitions (1902)
YAS Records Series Vol. 21	The Lay Subsidy of 1301 (1897)

Index of Personal Names and Place Names